What Presidents Are Made Of

To Janet

ATHENEUM BOOKS FOR YOUNG READERS
An imprint of Simon & Schuster Children's
Publishing Division
1230 Avenue of the Americas
New York, New York 10020
Text copyright © 2004, 2012 by Sarah L. Thomson
Illustrations copyright © 2004, 2012 by Hanoch Piven
All rights reserved, including the right of reproduction
in whole or in part in any form.
ATHENEUM BOOKS FOR YOUNG READERS is a
registered trademark of Simon & Schuster, Inc.
For information about special discounts for bulk
purchases, please contact Simon & Schuster Special
Sales at 1-866-506-1949 or
business@simonandschuster.com.
The Simon & Schuster Speakers Bureau can bring
authors to your live event. For more information or to
book an event, contact the Simon & Schuster Speakers
Bureau at 1-866-248-3049 or visit our website at
www.simonspeakers.com.
Also available in an Atheneum Books for Young Readers
hardcover edition
Book design by Ann Bobco
The text for this book is set in Centaur.
The illustrations for this book are rendered in paint on
plaster-covered wood adorned with glued-on objects.
Manufactured in China
1214 SCP
First Atheneum Books for Young Readers paperback
edition January 2012
10 9 8 7 6 5 4
The Library of Congress has cataloged the hardcover
edition as follows:
Piven, Hanoch.
What presidents are made of/Hanoch Piven.—1st ed.
p. cm.
ISBN 978-0-689-86880-1 (hc)
1. Presidents—United States—Biography—Juvenile
literature. 2. Presidents—United States—Portraits—
Juvenile literature. [1. Presidents.] I. Title.
E176 .I.P69 2004
973' .09'9—dc22 2003023579
ISBN 978-1-4424-4433-1 (pbk)
ISBN 978-1-4424-4520-8 (eBook)

SOURCES FOR QUOTATIONS

JACKSON: "I had a fight with Jackson . . ."
From Frederic A. Ogg. *The Reign of Andrew Jackson.* (New Haven, CT: 1919), page 31.

LINCOLN: "If I had another face . . ."
From Richard Hanser. "The Lincoln Who Lives in Anecdote," *Reader's Digest* LXXIV (February 1959), page 253.

ROOSEVELT, T.: "Get action . . ."
From Richard Hofstadter. *The American Political Tradition.* (New York: 1948), pages 210–211.

COOLIDGE: "You lose."
From Ishbel Ross, *Grace Coolidge and Her Era.* (New York: 1962), page 67.

KENNEDY: "It was involuntary. . . ."
From Paul F. Boller Jr., *Presidential Anecdotes.* (New York: 1981), page 299.

OBAMA: "He's confident, not afraid . . ."
From David Mendell, adapted by Sarah L. Thomson, *Obama: A Promise of Change* (New York: 2008), page 45.

BIBLIOGRAPHY

Bailey, Thomas A. *Presidential Saints and Sinners.* New York: The Free Press, 1981.
Boller, Paul F. Jr. *Presidential Anecdotes.* New York: Oxford University Press, 1981.
Conover, Carole. *Cover Girls: The True Story of Harry Conover.* New Jersey: Prentice-Hall, 1978.
Ivins, Molly, and Lou Dubose. *Shrub: The Short But Happy Political Life of George W. Bush.* New York: Random House, 2000.
Krull, Kathleen. *Lives of the Presidents: Fame, Shame, and What the Neighbors Thought.* San Diego: Harcourt Brace & Co., 1998.
Maraniss, David. *First In His Class: A Biography of Bill Clinton.* New York: Simon & Schuster, 1995.
Roosevelt, Elliott, and James Brough. *A Rendezvous With Destiny: The Roosevelts of the White House.* New York: Putnam, 1975.
Rubel, David. *Mr. President: The Human Side of America's Chief Executives.* Alexandria, VA: Time-Life Books, 1998.

TIMELINE PHOTOGRAPHS AND ILLUSTRATIONS CREDITS

what PRESIDENTS are made of

by
Hanoch Piven

ATHENEUM BOOKS FOR YOUNG READERS

New York

London

Toronto

Sydney

New Delhi

American presidents are great to draw because most have very distinctive faces and larger-than-life personalities. Lincoln's unique beard and serious gaze; Ronald Reagan's pompadour hair; Jimmy Carter's big, white smile; Clinton's puffy nose—they are not only references that are ingrained in our memory, but they somehow represent certain character traits of the men.

Objects are perfect building blocks for portraits. Each object has its own personality: white cotton "says" something different than a boxing glove; a square, angled steel ruler sends a different message than a marshmallow.

When matching objects to the "essence" of the presidents, I began to make funny associations: sometimes the pairings were logical and sometimes nonsensical, sometimes they evoked the "publicly known" character of the presidents, and, at other times, they related more to the specific anecdote told.

If I found an appropriate object that was not contemporary to the time of the depicted president, I "allowed" the object to live in the illustration, in the name of nonsense and fun. After all, this is not an encyclopedia, and Clinton's nose is not really a marshmallow.

You are encouraged to see how successful I was in rendering the presidents by comparing their illustrations to their actual pictures, which appear at the end of the book (although presidents tend to resemble their caricature more than themselves). And, of course, you are encouraged to try your own "object portraits" of the presidents.

—hanoch piven

George Washington was the first president of the United States. Abraham Lincoln ended slavery. Franklin D. Roosevelt led the United States during World War II.

But what were the presidents *like*? Did they make jokes? Did they play with their children?

Here's a look at the presidents, from George Washington to Barack Obama, in moments that don't usually make it into history books. Catch a glimpse of Washington fighting fires . . . or Clinton living life to the fullest . . . or Jimmy Carter helping the homeless. See the characters of the men who have lived in the White House. See what presidents are made of.

PRESIDENTS are made of

GOOD DEEDS

In GEORGE WASHINGTON's time, there was no fire department. If a house caught on fire, everyone nearby was supposed to help put it out. Just a few months before he died, at the age of sixty-seven, Washington was riding on his horse down the street when he heard that a fire had broken out near the market. He jumped off his horse and began to pump water to pour on the flames. When people saw the first president fighting the fire, they ran to help.

PRESIDENTS are made of

THOMAS JEFFERSON hated stuffy, formal manners. He wore shabby clothes and muddy boots inside the White House. Officials from other countries were shocked when he met them in his dressing gown and slippers. Jefferson even let his pet mockingbird fly free around the White House.

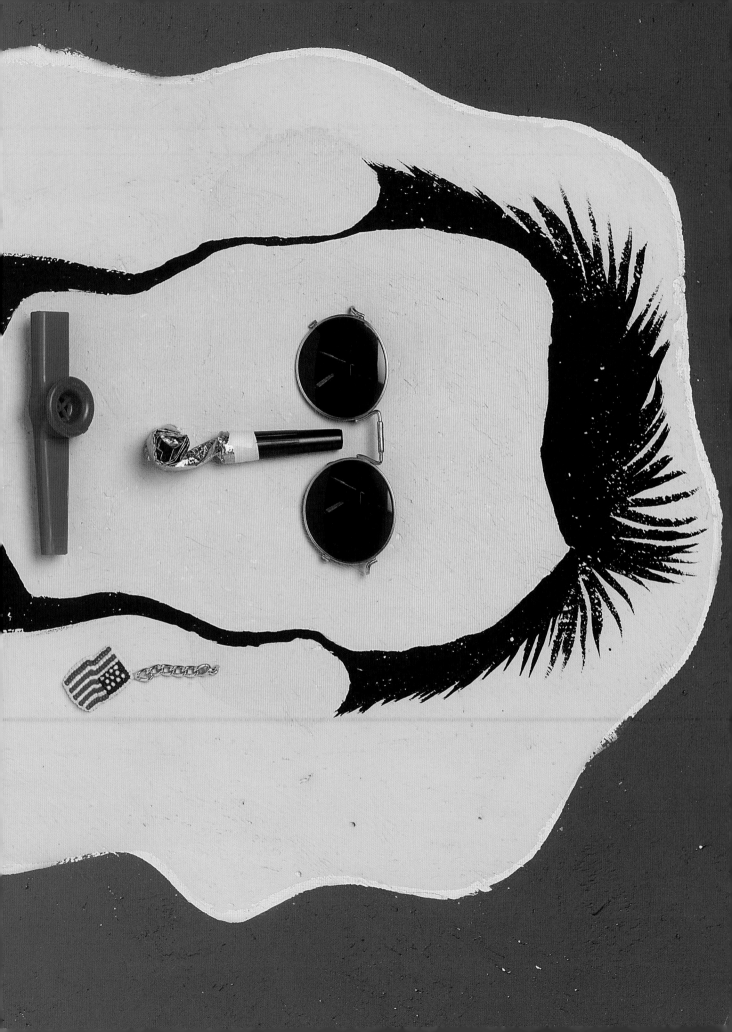

PRESIDENTS are made of

ULYSSES S. GRANT loved driving his one-horse carriage fast— sometimes a little *too* fast. One day a policeman, who didn't recognize the president, stopped him as he dashed through the streets of Washington and gave him a twenty-dollar fine for speeding. Grant paid the money and wrote a letter praising the policeman for doing his job so well.

PRESIDENTS are made of

THEODORE ROOSEVELT

studied judo, rode horses, rowed boats, played tennis, climbed mountains, and hunted in Africa. He had pillow fights and played hide-and-seek with his children (and he always wanted to be "it"). Roosevelt said, "Don't fritter away your time; create, act, take a place wherever you are and be somebody; get action."

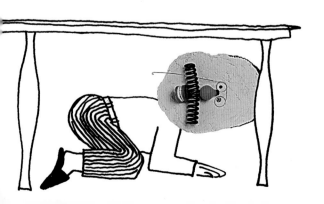

WILLIAM HOWARD TAFT, our heaviest president, weighed more than three hundred pounds (three times as much as our lightest president, James Madison). He was so big that he got stuck in the White House bathtub. Taft had a new one put in that weighed a ton and could hold four average-sized people. Many thought of Taft as jolly because of his size—like Santa Claus—but actually he was miserable being president. Afterward he became a judge on the Supreme Court, a job he liked much better.

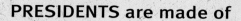

FUN AND GAMES

CALVIN COOLIDGE

said so little that his nickname was "Silent Cal." Once, a woman sitting next to him at dinner told Coolidge that she had made a bet she could get more than two words out of him. "You lose," he told her. But calm, quiet Coolidge rode a mechanical horse for exercise every morning, whooping like a cowboy.

PRESIDENTS
are
made
of

PICKY EATING

Even though FRANKLIN D. ROOSEVELT was president, he couldn't control what he was served for meals. The White House housekeeper was a terrible cook and insisted on making things he hated, like broccoli. Even a special occasion didn't mean she'd serve fancy food. For a luncheon celebrating Roosevelt's re-election, she offered chicken salad, rolls without butter, and cake without frosting! But Roosevelt couldn't bring himself to fire her. He would just fix himself an egg salad sandwich if he was still hungry after a meal.

PRESIDENTS are made of

LIFE SAVERS

JOHN F. KENNEDY served in the navy during World War II, and his boat was sunk by a Japanese ship. Kennedy saved a wounded soldier's life by taking the end of the man's life jacket between his teeth and towing him through the water to an island three miles away.

When he was later asked how he became a war hero, Kennedy answered, "It was absolutely involuntary. They sank my boat."

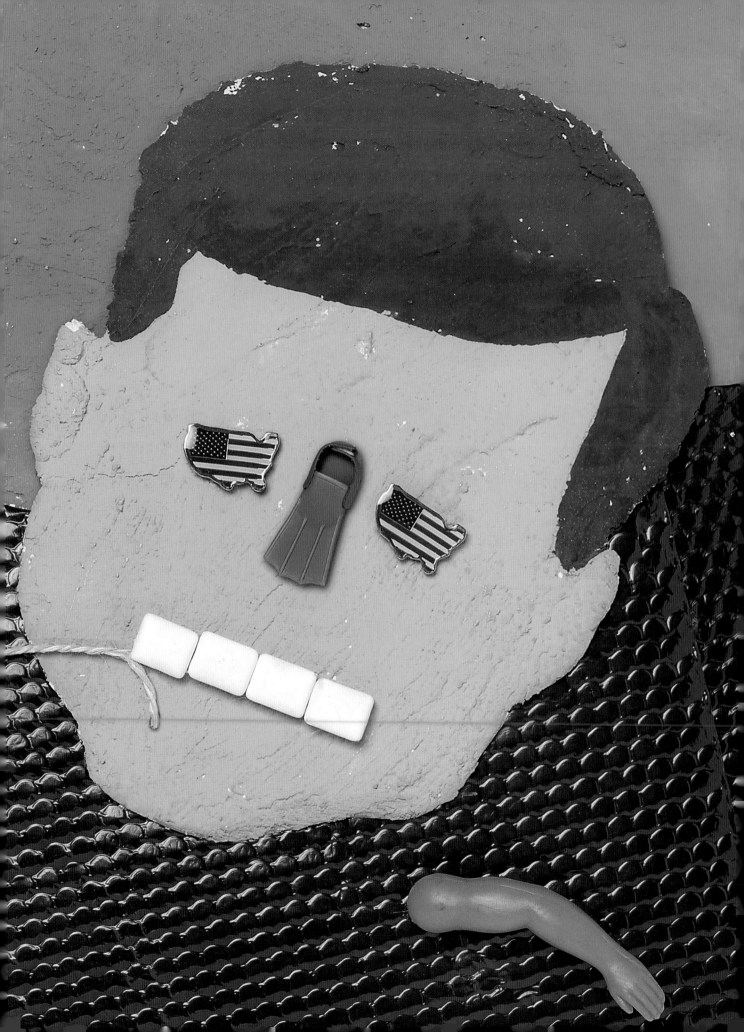

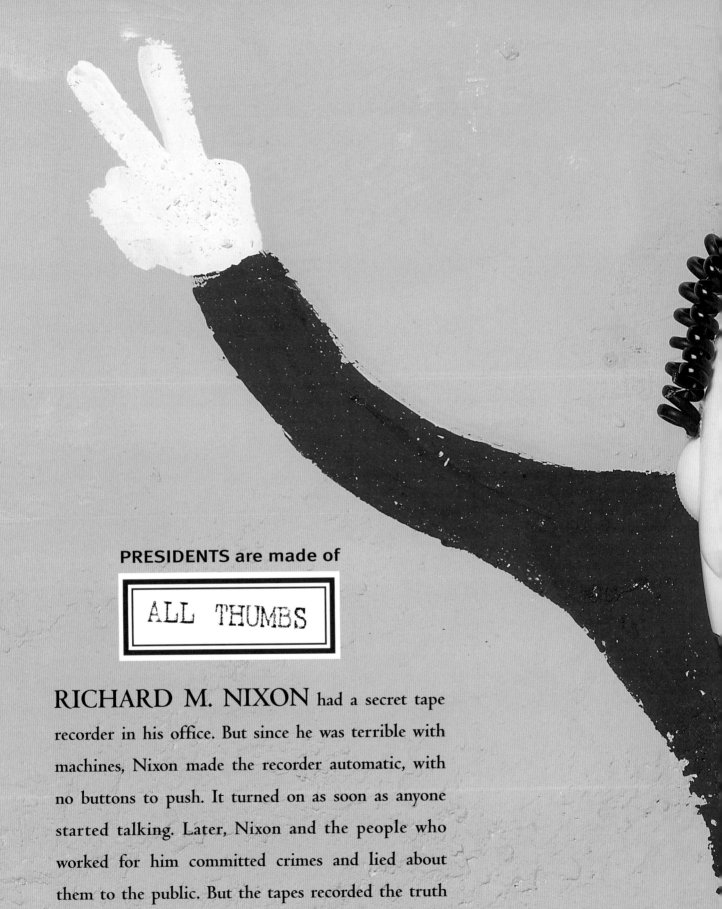

PRESIDENTS are made of

ALL THUMBS

RICHARD M. NIXON had a secret tape recorder in his office. But since he was terrible with machines, Nixon made the recorder automatic, with no buttons to push. It turned on as soon as anyone started talking. Later, Nixon and the people who worked for him committed crimes and lied about them to the public. But the tapes recorded the truth about what had actually happened. Those tapes forced Nixon to resign and leave the White House.

PRESIDENTS are made of GLAMOUR

Years before he became president (and before he married his wife), GERALD R. FORD, a handsome former football star, dated a model. Together the two of them posed for a ski weekend layout called "A Weekend in the Life of the Beautiful People," in *Look* magazine. Ford had a copy of the magazine, but, as he said, "It's not something you flaunt around the house."

PRESIDENTS are made of

HELPING HANDS

Helping people is important to **JIMMY CARTER.** He taught Sunday School while president, and afterward he decided to spend his time doing good for others. Carter travels around the world trying to make peace between countries, and one week every year, he builds houses for the homeless for an organization called Habitat for Humanity International.

PRESIDENTS are made of | SWEET STUFF

RONALD REAGAN
loved jelly beans and kept a jar on his
desk to share (but he tried to keep his
favorites, the coconut ones, for himself).

Reagan was the first movie star to become president. After college he worked in radio and then the movies, and soon became famous. In one movie, *Bedtime for Bonzo,* he starred with a chimpanzee. Reagan used part of the money he made making movies to buy his parents a house.

PRESIDENTS are made of

GEORGE BUSH met his wife, Barbara, at a dance. He wanted to get to know the woman in the red-and-green dress, but he was too embarrassed to ask her to dance, so they just talked. At their wedding George finally danced with Barbara but warned her that she'd better enjoy it—he would never dance in public again.

PRESIDENTS are made of ENTHUSIASM

BILL CLINTON does everything full tilt. He loves to eat. People have seen him chew up an apple in a few bites—skin, core, seeds, and all—and gobble an entire pie without even using a fork.

He also loves to read, to play jazz saxophone, and to talk. One of his teachers in grade school even gave him a C for raising his hand too often.

PRESIDENTS are made of **SPORTS FANS**

GEORGE W. BUSH is the first president to have owned a baseball team. Before he was president, he bought a share in the Texas Rangers. Bush loves baseball, but he didn't buy the team just for fun. He paid less than a million dollars for his share and sold it later for more than fifteen million.

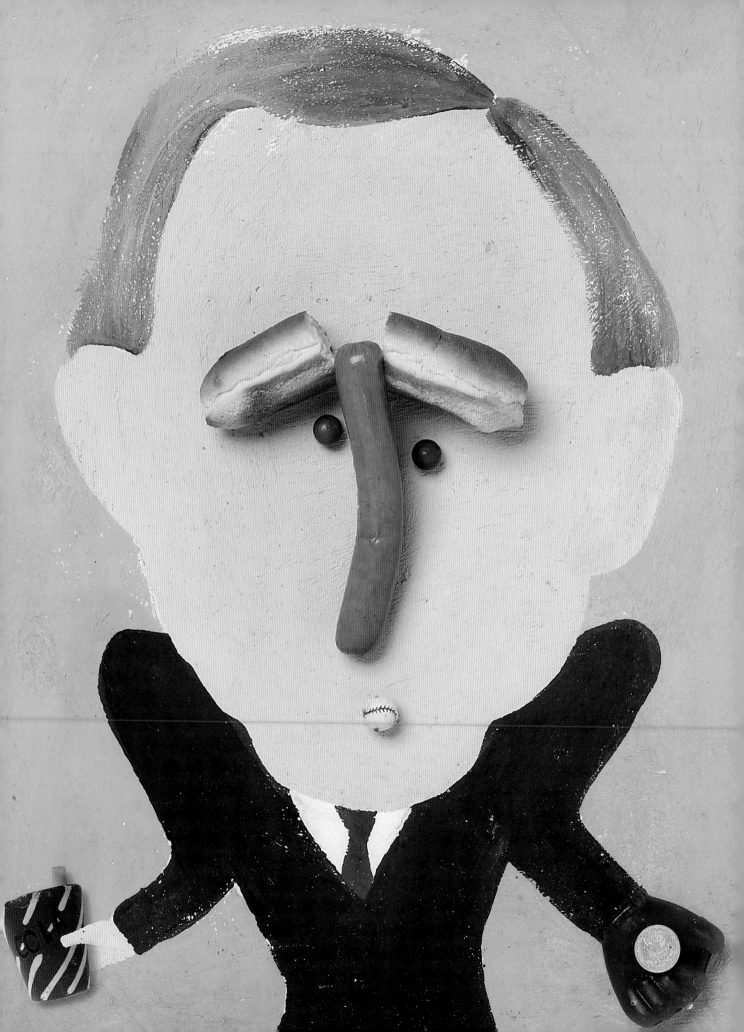

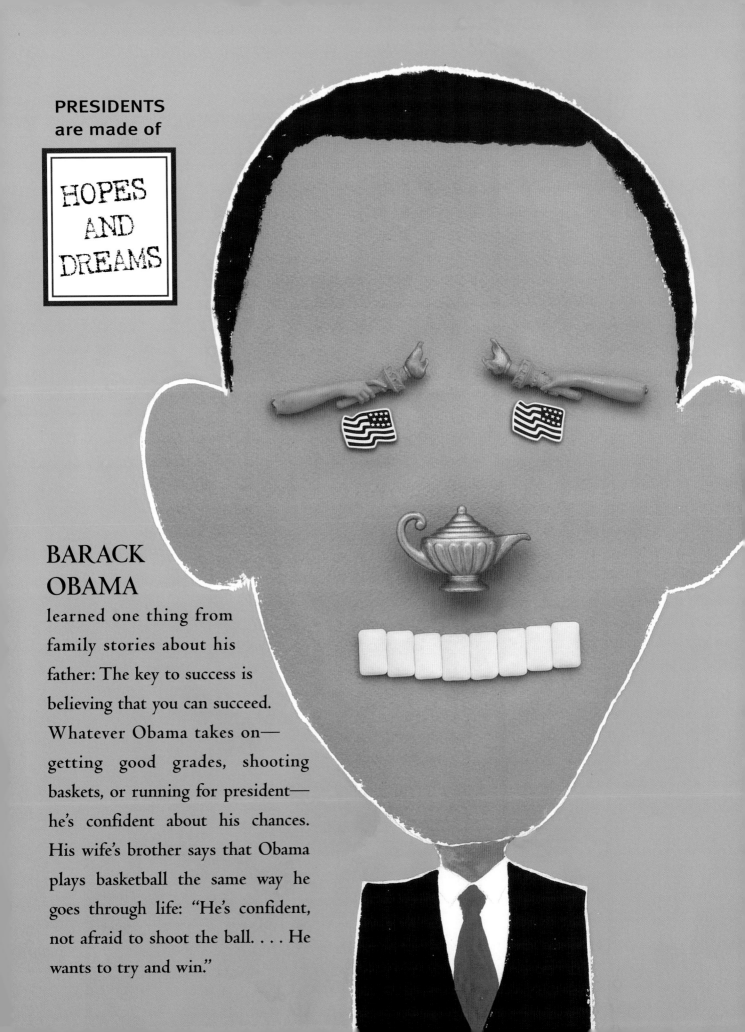

PRESIDENTS
are made of

HOPES
AND
DREAMS

BARACK OBAMA

learned one thing from family stories about his father: The key to success is believing that you can succeed. Whatever Obama takes on— getting good grades, shooting baskets, or running for president— he's confident about his chances. His wife's brother says that Obama plays basketball the same way he goes through life: "He's confident, not afraid to shoot the ball. . . . He wants to try and win."

A Presidential Timeline

from
GEORGE
WASHINGTON

GEORGE
WASHINGTON ⭐

b. 1732, d. 1799
1789–1797 (years in office)

JOHN ADAMS

b. 1735, d. 1826
1797–1801 (years in office)

THOMAS
JEFFERSON ⭐

b. 1742, d. 1826
1801–1809 (years in office)

JAMES
MADISON

b. 1751, d. 1836
1809–1817 (years in office)

JAMES
MONROE

b. 1758, d. 1831
1817–1825 (years in office)

JOHN
QUINCY
ADAMS

b. 1767, d. 1848
1825–1829 (years in office)

ANDREW
JACKSON ⭐

b. 1767, d. 1845
1829–1837 (years in office)

MARTIN
VAN BUREN

b. 1782, d. 1862
1837–1841 (years in office)

WILLIAM
HENRY
HARRISON

b. 1773, d. 1841
March 1841–April 1841
(1 month in office)

JOHN TYLER

b. 1790, d. 1862
1841–1845 (years in office)

JAMES K.
POLK

b. 1795, d. 1849
1845–1849 (years in office)

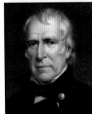

ZACHARY
TAYLOR

b. 1784, d. 1850
1849–1850 (years in office)

MILLARD
FILLMORE

b. 1800, d. 1874
1850–1853 (years in office)

FRANKLIN
PIERCE

b. 1804, d. 1869
1853–1857 (years in office)

JAMES
BUCHANAN

b. 1791, d. 1868
1857–1861 (years in office)

ABRAHAM
LINCOLN ⭐

b. 1809, d. 1865
1861–1865 (years in office)

ANDREW
JOHNSON

b. 1808, d. 1875
1865–1869 (years in office)

ULYSSES S.
GRANT ⭐

b. 1822, d. 1885
1869–1877 (years in office)

RUTHERFORD B
HAYES

b. 1822, d. 1893
1877–1881 (years in office)

JAMES A.
GARFIELD

b. 1831, d. 1881
Mar. 1881–Sept. 1881
(6 months in office)

CHESTER A.
ARTHUR

b. 1830, d. 1886
1881–1885 (years in office)

- - -→ **to BARACK OBAMA**

A Presidential Timeline

RICHARD M. NIXON ⭐

b. 1913, d. 1994
1969 1974 (years in office)

GROVER CLEVELAND

b. 1837, d. 1908
1885–1889;
1893–1897 (years in office)

CALVIN COOLIDGE ⭐

b. 1872, d. 1933
1923–1929 (years in office)

GERALD R. FORD ⭐

b. 1913, d. 2006
1974–1977 (years in office)

BENJAMIN HARRISON

b. 1833, d. 1901
1889–1893 (years in office)

HERBERT HOOVER

b. 1874, d. 1964
1929–1933 (years in office)

JIMMY CARTER ⭐

b. 1924
1977–1981 (years in office)

WILLIAM McKINLEY

b. 1843, d. 1901
1897–1901 (years in office)

FRANKLIN D. ROOSEVELT ⭐

b. 1882, d. 1945
1933–1945 (years in office)

RONALD REAGAN ⭐

b. 1911, d. 2004
1981–1989 (years in office)

THEODORE ROOSEVELT ⭐

b. 1858, d. 1919
1901–1909 (years in office)

HARRY S. TRUMAN

b. 1884, d. 1972
1945–1953 (years in office)

GEORGE BUSH ⭐

b. 1924
1989–1993 (years in office)

WILLIAM HOWARD TAFT ⭐

b. 1857, d. 1930
1909–1913 (years in office)

DWIGHT D. EISENHOWER

b. 1890, d. 1969
1953–1961 (years in office)

WILLIAM JEFFERSON CLINTON ⭐

b. 1946
1993–2001 (years in office)

WOODROW WILSON

b. 1856, d. 1924
1913–1921 (years in office)

JOHN F. KENNEDY ⭐

b. 1917, d. 1963
1961–1963 (years in office)

GEORGE W. BUSH ⭐

b. 1946
2001–2009 (years in office)

WARREN G. HARDING

b. 1865, d. 1923
1921–1923 (years in office)

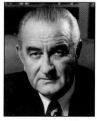

LYNDON B. JOHNSON

b. 1908, d. 1973
1963–1969 (years in office)

BARACK OBAMA ⭐

b. 1961
2009– (years in office)

⭐ Presidents illustrated in this book